compass
bearing

Poems

Per Wästberg

translated by
Hildred Crill

compass
bearing

Poems

Per Wästberg

translated by
Hildred Crill

MARICK PRESS

LIBRARY OF CONGRESS CATALOGUING
IN PUBLICATION DATA
Wästberg, Per
Poems. Translations. English.
Compass Bearing/ Per Wästberg
ISBN: 978-1-934851-46-3

Design and typesetting by HSDesigns
Cover design by HSDesigns
Cover image: HSDesigns
Printed and bound in the United States.

Marick Press
P.O. Box 36253
Grosse Pointe Farms
Michigan 48236
www.marickpress.com

Distributed by spdbooks.org and Ingram

MARICK PRESS

Acknowledgments:

Thanks to *Ars Interpres* where some of the poems first appeared.

CONTENTS

BEGINNING

Dawn in time-high grass.
Reality untested:
I didn't skim the surface
but plunged into its cavities,
twisted in its fibers.
I laid glowworms in a cup
and dug up the seagull's year-old grave
curious about everything that was transformed.
Like deathwatch beetles in old timber
I worked my way into the world I got.
And reality, grateful for the attention,
arranged itself into a landscape and a home.

WEEKDAY

Boil beets, chop onions, take the key from the nail,
go down cellar for winter potatoes.
Write in the journal: "Overcast. Went to bed late.
Fixed the kick-sled."
Put useless coins in the piggy bank.
Count empty bottles. Brood, startle
at the main road's rattle, hear psalm song:
next door a traveling preacher has a revival.

Want to be someone else, want to know something more.
Test the night-thin ice for the sake of trying.
Charge this ordinariness with still more watts
so unexpected light burns through the varnish.
Tempted to give this verse a deeper angle as well
and distrust the motif's ability to bear weight.
Still – undertones are overflow.
The ice holds over black water.

QUESTIONNAIRE

If I think it was better before?
I haven't gone so far that I have
a before. Hope it gets better later.
Illness, divorce, odd children, grief
and a breakneck vertigo in the world's unbalance—
be prepared for everything! But I'm not prepared.
I withdraw from the storms, I want to adjust
The Barometer in Kalmar, that will do.

Museum

The goose feather Grandmother picked her ear with.
The mug with pens by the cashbook.
A rocking chair for no one.
Dolls: Regina von Emmeritz was the grandest.
Paintings: one made of wood, not planed on the back,
a pound of paint, 2 ½ feet by 2.
Father, Mother, Sister.
Dead, weightless, soon I will be also.
Someone will stare from the wall at some others.
Some others will believe someone lived happy
or so-so. The nice eyes
run in our family.

What more to point out in the family museum?
The black globe. No lands or seas,
nowhere to set out for, only latitudes and longitudes.
In the geographic net and still not caught by it:
yellow and white seabirds.

DOUBLE EXPOSURE

I pressed the steel nib hard against the paper
to produce a simple and strong contour.
With that, the point bent back and split
and the writing became blurred and double:
two versions, one of which is
the other's shadow and pursuer.

When I read the text, I grow uncertain
of its import. On which point shall I stand?
Words don't let themselves be speared. More fleeting
contact is what the paper should be exposed to.
I try to have a light touch – but too late!
I can't lessen the gulf between the point's halves.
It widens more and more.

TIMETABLE

We make signs to each other.
We are signs to each other.
Today becomes tomorrow yesterday.
We have to do everything now
and still leave everything undone.
We have to say everything
without betraying the unsayable.

The night capsizes. The sky is arched
gray blue like a seabird's egg.
Floating in Cardan suspension, though that's before Polhem,
the Earth rests in its space.

The simple is part of the difficult to interpret,
of a contradictory program—
as when the wick of a candle is split,
one strand becomes quickly charred,
the other burns as before.

Determination of Place

Snow melt...water and grit...
Cranes plow over time's magic valley:
the movement immeasurable according to Einstein
because no one knows its point of departure.
Existence without a fence.

On the seesaw: today and tomorrow.
Roads heavily trod. Nights like dark
mineral. No signs of welcome.
Small answers for big questions:
It doesn't get worse, it doesn't get
better than this.

Most things are given the wrong names.
The postal receipt counts like your own.
The Wagoner in his constellation drops
some burning buttons.
The beetle cleans his narrow tooth.
On a cucumber leaf somewhere
a place awaits us.

In the Land of Egypt

One evening when the words flutter homeless like the mosquitoes
he recalls a brown-paneled compartment on the route Luxor-
Cairo. A woman spoke to him in unguarded quiet,
injured like a reprimanded school child. Her glance
of thin neon read him like a letter and she touched
him, playfully, with ardent stillness. He was without compass,
unprepared. Egg bread in her bag, nescafé and cognac in his,
medicine for a short passage. Openness of strangers in a cabin
with a broken light bulb, weak radio batteries, between need
and cry. The improper is punished in a later eternity.
She was in flight. Her lips were opened by an unseen
chisel, her heels rubbed by the sandal's edging.
Desire surged with the train's motion. The circumstances
had their own will. Attentive dermis. Nipples,
aspen leaves stained with copper. His body pried open dizzy, hers
colorlessly alone, yet not sealed shut: an untracked grief.

With a breath hard as iron she drew
her escape route against his back and loins.
Let him open glades, canals and
her dark floodgate, let him seek in worn murmurings
hollows, farther and farther in, farther and farther away,
indelicately like an earwig, eagerly as when
someone packs a knapsack in haste, against all the rules.
Her tongue's aftertaste of salt and alder and ooze.
That was not love, not history—
and the arrival to Cairo greatly delayed.
Unreadable names, desolate sand surfaces, a dung fire in a village

were their interval between juncture and chance.
He fell asleep between the stations,
unharmed encased in her where the pulse
throbbed insatiable, inconsolable.

DREAM LIFE

My dreams are entirely abstract now.
I never fly from the window ledge,
meet a rhinoceros on the spiral staircase,
lie turned upside-down with unknown women.
I'm never reached by the blasphemous messages
from Sunday school's basement.
Something of importance has been lost.

Dear Professor Freud,
the fault fissure has closed up.
I can't even find a pit to be sucked down into.
My excellent Mr. Jung,
the archetypes have abandoned me.
My secret fauna is extinct: brook-swan,
and lynx-sandpiper, balsamic stair-fowl –
these wild illiterates that were catalogued
once by my dreams' squint-eyed assistant.
Could I make an appointment with Dr. Hartnagel, refugee
from Vienna, renowned therapist, who with a finger
erect in the psychosomatic storm gives grief
this good form and gets us to recall the rocking horse
in the playroom at a remote alpine hotel.

As it is now, I work my way forward
night after night to the same mathematical solution.
I bore my way through the shell of prevailing norms.
Among white papers' figures, strokes and signs
I catch a glimpse of the most intricate of formulas.
Filled with costly confusion, in a trembling introspective
second, I stand on the threshold of the universal mystery.
My heart pounds with abashed pride.
A risky venture succeeded. What does it matter now
that death is a few seconds nearer?

I wake up exhausted. The formula is crossed out
in the same moment I write it.
An imageless dream, filled with prime numbers:
nothing to remember. First despair,
then an absentmindedness that sees the day out.
So the evening comes with a lost hope.
It's like the time in an earlier dream I received
a vital prescription in an envelope
and my fingers were too numb to open it.

WINTER BREAK

If I could write a tribute to the eraser
for nine crowns from Järvsö Book & Paper.
It smells of lemon and looks like an ace of spades.
My son carries it home happy.

Thirty-five years ago in the same jumbled shop
which surely no one has inventoried since
I bought an everlasting notepad.
We wrote with a nail on a scent of aniline.
The cellophane buckled. The reverse side remained
and to take apart the machinery. What short-lived
eternity! Nevertheless the writing's still there.

When he sees an ace of spades and senses the taste
of lemon, he'll remember the winter inn's
corridors, icy ski runs, the final in ping pong and
the hat parade, though the eraser has erased itself
and eternity come to an end.

Displaced Time

1

Ramses II on temporary loan to Musée de l'Homme.
The brittle bandage has kept his passions in check.
His skin has the scent of raisins and old books.
Rescued out of timelessness, helplessly reused,
he becomes an experimental field. Millennia
have been stored in his body. The frequency
of the molecules is calculated in his kneecaps.

Concerning the essential, he lets us hover in uncertainty.
He is neither then nor now, neither alive nor dead.
A dried fence between the Upper Kingdom's statistics
and our own database.

2

I go to sleep on one floor, wake up on another.
I've disappointed someone—but who?
Elsa Björkman-Goldschmidt (with the look of Karin Boye),
pageboy cut, white collar with black rosette.
"Please, Elsa, what are you doing by my bed?"
She busies herself with her papers, keeping silent.
Elsa's voice: "I sentence you to life."
I understand: to another life, hers.
I'm not alarmed. I answer.
"I'll read the book I got from you, later."

She walks around my bed, painfully upright.
She asks: "Which relatives should I inform?"
Many. But I can't think which.
I look at her with renewed interest.
Just like that, I know she is dead.

CHARADE

I don't know if language helps me to see.
I dread the scentless process of soul-searching.
I live on an advance from an unwilling consul.
I convey the faint smell of blown out candles.
I use old-time soaps, pale as a flounder's belly.
I have a tin box with a strap that locks up the jaws of the dead.
I exchange old age's muskrat coat for the blank false leads of early
    summer.
I imagine I stand on forbidden ground; from that, my desire to travel.
I mark the leading line toward the unpredictable and forget
how the spirit in the binnacle sets the compass bearing.
In the chaos scientist's unbalance I divine the perplexing lightness of
    being.
I've misplaced my flute made out of a fly's leg—
and in no other way will I make myself known.

WATER OF DARKNESS, CLEAR

1

Early in life we all look like each other,
the sweet pea sprout is a fetus with a bulging forehead.
I: a semi-product, a transparent jellyfish
rocking on other people's seas.
We move between colossal algae
far under the level of daylight.

The nursemaid has hands smooth with Vaseline.
A pre-Christian fragrance of unaired mattresses,
shriveled crabapples and fleas in a matchbox.
The prunes swell in boiling water.
The family albums' glue-dry scandals are caught
in the streak of light under the double doors.

"A slacker! A rascal! A poor excuse for a boy!"
The walking stick clatters on the gravel, the neck tight.
Someone passes away, a figure vanishes.
Summer dusk. Reality distorted.
The water surface is drawn together with a thread.
No mosquito nets protect against the stings of the past.

2

June is June. The white currants never turn black.
Time's bones are brittle
and the cold bath house in a deplorable state.
Insurance for longhorn beetle not paid.
The cuckoo calls from a large saucepan.
Under a thinned sky we dip
into sweetness of overripe fruit.
The self-analytical shadows pass
over the spirit level's blind eye.

We offer intrigues, skirmishes,
cousins half asleep. In a basement cubbyhole
there are flags torn apart by the wind,
worthless German bills, the peat factory's
stock certificates in a green cardboard box.
The daughters' fragile nerves turn the pages to
a new episode in the family's serial story.

3

As when a well-thumbed book opens to a certain page
I recognize my early years:
winter's wake through summer, the specks of dust
in an untouched whirl, the clack of backgammon checkers,
Roman numerals stiff as soldiers.
The swing's waterlogged rope creaks between the trees
and there's Polyphemos, the giant,
gap between front teeth,
inner arms white as skimmed milk,
arch creased with an imprint of earth.

In the cupboard closest to the ceiling, congratulatory notes,
tennis scores and The Woman's Periods.
Harmless dust jackets for crafts and boat mechanics
disguise the Misses von Pahlen.
In the Citizen's Guide, brown with gold lettering,
I look up Bankruptcy, Rape
and Binding Conditions.

Passion is wave crests on the sea of indifference.
Here devoted distance prevails,
ecstasy under rigorous etiquette.
You secure lukewarm wash water in an enameled bucket
and amiable replies to letters.
Spots on the handles of forks are cleaned carefully away.

Fingers grope under a rough tabletop.
The chandelier ball drops into the soup tureen
when it thunders one evening in August.
The troublesome guest leaves behind

unsigned accounts and a rejected application
for a license: traces of a melodrama without weight.

The golden pendulum swings
and the beige wings of the thrush beat.
The light becomes thin like a metacarpal bone.
Soon you are no one and nowhere.

4

These distant rooms that smell of coolness,
we mix them up over time.
What we lose is not time
but room after room.
We float through the houses
where we once lived
and they have no names.

5

Here autumn coalesces with summer
in a surge of dizzying leaves.
The fire grows cold in the mirror's gleam.
The hothouse windows fill with mud.
Around our endless breakfasts, lone swims,
the world is framed in lead.
Fox fur spread over marble floors.
Creak from unoiled hinges. Yet no door.
Light bulbs burnt out.
But the madonna's teeth gleam.

6

Meek as a dace, destitute as a clear-cut acre,
she arrived to take care of the household.
She scrubbed the rust stripes in the washbasin.
I did nothing.
"You wouldn't even move a muscle
if your own mother died before your eyes."

I don't forget her face like a termite's
with her pinched mouth – as if she still
had needles between her lips.
"How would the world look
if everyone wrote left-handed?"
I have waited for the answer my whole life.
She pushed a scrap of paper, white and delayed,
under the door of the future.

7

Leaping between freedom and leash
I rubbed a pebble in my pocket
to wear out my thumbprints.
History was a sky on the inside of the cranium
and the world an unfamiliar jewel.
I observed it
and waited for time
to take a serious turn.

8

I saw the floors scoured with the breath of the vanished;
the knot-holes, eyes of predators with no whites in them.
The shadows remained in dark notebooks.
I made my way into the night's parlor,
I searched among the dreams' utensils
and found a recipe for emptiness:
water, instant flour, the crust of a discarded loaf
are blended to a death mask for a kinsman.

A course of shallow events filled my days then
but above them the indistinct high tension networks,
below them those ungodly gushes from the body's interior.
It hammered like in a long shut off waterworks
and I breathed carefully to soften the pain.
I sought accommodation for an unworn feeling.
I wanted to fall asleep in the crook of summer's arm
against a skin of brightest sand.

9

Some have nowhere to go.
What remains in the room
is what could not be removed.

A childhood sunk in chronological shadow,
the fire's reflection on dull parquet.
Hands groping for a napkin or a knee,
the words remembered what the body had forgotten,
the child sat there in the corner, thin as a stork's bill.
In the pachisi's circles, the gazes
from bodies of roadkill gleamed.
The meltwater from our lives drained away
with a slurping sound like when horses drink,
invisible in the twilight.

10

From the war I remember a blacked out café
and the Sassnitz ferry that had stopped running.
Mussolini's bulging eyes and the smell
in the telegraph office stairwell, the editor of the local paper
with his nicotine stained fingers around the red pen,
the bent music stand at the city hotel and
feigned attacks at the billiard table, desk lids
scratched by penknives. And someone wept
in every room in the house except mine.

I was ripe stagnation
and my hand heavy as a stone block.

I remember the school cap's blue and yellow lining,
a card deck's smell of hand sweat and schnapps,
the rigid swan necks of the searchlights
over a horizon stretched to a breaking point,
the gate's spikes of black-painted iron,
the drying loft warm and oxygen-poor,
the soft thuds of plums in the evening fog and a silence
powerful as tracks of heavy shoes in the snow.

I remember the ice, brown as frozen tea,
the sack of firewood outside the door and parcels
too large for the mailbox,
the Russian boy, a refugee with the strange name Kolya,
and a Jewish tailor who did alterations on Döbeln Street,
his eyebrows lustrous as velvet
and a warning finger against umber-colored wallpaper;
the walls were thin as a child's arteries.
We were all on someone's list.

I remember the gasmasks on the hatrack,
the cycle patrol in the night, free time between lessons
and the future's hollow face.
It was to be continued in the sequel. And the consequences continued.

11

The Greek alphabet was formed like cranes in flight.
I am an open book that has fallen apart into sheets and odd
pages. Someone has cleaned his nails with my corners.
Glue my spine, give me a cover to hold together
the one who can be me.
The copyright belongs to someone else.

12

The power of those who describe is great.
They mark out sunken islands,
indicate a forgotten shipwreck,
a feldspar mine with the sign
"work of men which later on closed down."
The maps, spread out, are numerous enough
to suffocate the world.
But they do not cover it.

Nothing was planned ahead,
it got to become what it became.
The terrain full of memories not rolled out.
But we know where we are
because we got lost here before.
In a moment we step into a story
where no one will find us.

13

In my landscape there are more trees than there are forests.
Memory is a tree ringed in by fallen fruit.
Staples hold eddying years in check.
First at a distance, the vicinity is visible.
I travel in a circle to avoid arriving.

Because I know something about the moment's firm ground
and these exposed seconds
that no dream can fence in:
how they glisten like drops of water
on the very end of an oar's blade.

What is, I see, has been made
of what is not.
The invisible infiltrates more and more.
The stone's capillaries breathe.
The gathered darkness rises.
The temporary's essence makes records important
though the pattern as a whole stays unexplored.

The unknown is where freedom is.
In the heart, vertigo creeps nearer to its edge.

ON LOVE

1

You stand on the pier,
its posts vanish into the deep water.
Invisible currents pull under the surface.
The rope is scorched around the bollard
by the ocean's skill.
The approach channel between beacons
finally finds the breakwater's sheltering boulder.
Contact with land. Wood chips. Tar.
A fragrance brought back. I moor.
Chance knew what it was doing.

_____

2

Every morning at breakfast 8:11 sharp I heard
your train to the city pass the viaduct over the highway.
I felt you looked in my direction.
The window catches sang that you existed,
I wondered what you'd do that day
and if we'd get to spend a single night together.

I knew how quickly you put on your coat
and how late you came to each meeting.
You wore a bird around your throat you bought for yourself
and a ring around your finger that you got from your husband.
I hid in you like in a writing desk's secret compartment.

The Mayan culture counted 584 days in a year:
the orbit of Venus around the Earth.
When I look out through the kitchen window
I glimpse you with the trash on the way to work.
Once more the time is 8:11.
Tie a knot in your handkerchief, my darling,
though you belong to the office culture
that jots figures perpetually on the palm of the hand.

Because now we've slept together
three thousand and one nights
and told everything that has happened
in as many days.
The bird has flown away,
the ring is replaced and the children grown.
You arrive late as usual
but you come all the same and you stay.

3

Quiet conversation one evening at the kitchen table.
The apples chilled by melting snow,
the cheese dusted with wholesome mold.
A domestic scene after a hard day.
The weariness rubbed away.
The dusk makes our gaze brighten.
Now we are, my beloved,
in the leaf-thin light.
The words float on calm wings.
Our hands move toward each other
assured of rest.
Nothing to write about.
Much to live in.

4

Thin airmail sheets
folded so many times
the words have become illegible.
In the folds love gathers
like the scraps
at the bottom of my back pocket.

5

I have a kindred spirit
in love's herb, Sedum telephium.
It protects itself with thick leaves
against long drought
to one day be saturated with trust.
If you had wanted
I would have come to you
even through the sewers.

6

With you I understand something
I don't grasp in myself.
With you I retrieve a lost time.
Inside you I enter an illuminated city.
With my eyes shut, I draw its map
so I'll find my way out of you
without losing you.

7

Your hands smell of topsoil, domestic life.
Your skin has the warmth held by a thermos.
No need to awaken desire
to remind me of you.
I yield to you
like an animal in evening-high grass.
We breathe out of rhythm
to come nearer to each other.
I don't want to love you
in any other form.
I live in a confidence
out of step with the times, slow
as our unfinished embrace.

8

The sound of the potter's wheel can be evoked again,
the breaking voices of the catastrophes,
the light carved into stone.
The labels come loose from rounded glass.
Radio signals reach us from unmanned stars.
A solution pursues its mystery to come into being.

A gust of wind on a calm day.
A touch, quick as meltwater.
As when with your fingertip
you search for the pulse
against the child's wrist bone.
Nearness is our room
while the icy wind combs Berenike's hair.

If I could speak with you
only in light vowels...
I discover new wrinkles on your face
like writing scraped out
from under another message.
"I found myself that time near
something unknown and unknowable
which I nonetheless had in my hand."

As when alabaster loses its dark core
in the fire's heat
and grows transparent—

9

One evening when the birds are screeching
like overtired children
and the shadows grasp the roots of the trees
and the wind is as stiff as a paintbrush,
there's a glimpse of a text in a foreign language.
We can't read it
although we grasp what it says.

10

Preserve love
in a vial in a molar tooth.
Some day
at an unavoidable moment
swallow it
and die.

LANDSCAPE

Over the sea a light travels that is filtered through deep forests.
The air is thin as though it could break.
We are movable stones on a map the wind creases.

The seasons distribute their signs like the butter-yellow
tiles in mahjong. The Earth's surface is a rough coat sleeve.
Leniency is decreed. The ax doesn't forget the tree.

In last year's reeds the spirit of the previous summer lives on.
The carrot sits too far down on the snowman.
Every sign needs another one to interpret it.

The spring ice cracks. Smoke from a driftwood fire.
The snow thins around cartilage-white skeletons of birds.
Silence is there like an old-fashioned murmur.

Not a sound. But the air listens to the arrow cast
of light into spring beech forest. In the cocoon
the butterfly awaits the next station: disembarking only.

A moist sun slips on the chimney caps.
But instinct knows the Rembrandt light lies.
Weather has no history, forgetfulness no color.

June is the shortest of months. Honeysuckle wakens
first in the twilight hour, when the wind brakes and branches
make a click as when a seat belt unbuckles.

Thoughts gather like livestock in the evening.
The gnats hover above the cool perch depth.
The flock of starlings takes off, a sooty firework.

The road whitens against the night, lips of the sea stacks smile.
The magpie nips a butterfly in flight toward Hablingbo.
Death ages with us. But it doesn't survive us.

The road to Öja has no traffic. A clock beats inside the whitebeam
    tree.
The horses of the Apocalypse clatter under the sofa bed's lid.
I hold ruin on tight reins.

When the sun sinks cloudberry-yellow in Näs, I drive the region
home, the wind turbines stop, the organ is blasted,
seething and blessed. Over the mainland the thunderstorm gets ready.

The boar from Fide breeding station is transported by trailer,
shrieks and roars in it, then a long silence.
It is the world's grief, not the breeder, that's out traveling.

August 10. The swallows full grown. A reconnaissance plane over
Hoburgen. No threat from Russia. Jupiter and Venus
on either side of Gotland. The sea is covered with a thin skin of light.

In sunny weather, Hemse center is beautiful too.
The library sells off *Cinnamoncandy* for ten crowns
and the only traffic light, outside the liquor store, has got stuck.

In the hammock between pear tree and whitebeam, I see
the stars: pale cherries, out of reach of the thrushes.
Let them never ripen. Let me avoid being spat out.

The jellyfish drift in their life jackets from coastal land
to coastal land seeking nutrient-rich soil.
Some day they will close their parasols and settle down.

The laughing gulls grow quiet in the late summer evening. Music
from open windows. The night has more time than the day:
a dark table we serve stories on.

Sometimes the summer recedes already in August.
A dry point scratches the sky's lead ceiling and the mosquitoes thicken
like fog over the marsh. No one knows if we'll meet until spring.

There are uninvented surfaces, inner hiking trails.
The tall poplars change the wind to notes.
Outside the day is as clear as a sail.

Country churches receive us like old aunts who haven't
been visited for a long time. No one genuflects before the altar
where the thistledown swirls along the floor in the draft from the sacristy.

Far off someone is planing in a shed, with a regular stroke.
Motion without frenzy and craving: like being embraced by sleep.
A dark cloud spreads slowly out on the hillside.

I moor the veranda that has come loose from the house. The sky
a marbled paper from a schoolbook. The girls blooming over
the grass, low voices, sunblock's SPF on their legs. Evening soon.

The summer ends with dewberries, harder than mouse droppings,
a pipit struck by the hawk, stubbled fields on fire.
The cat buried, the Apollo bicycle locked in the barn.

Albums with family photos are piled up at the flea market.
Lives, for sale; they held together once and were split apart.
Piano playing, petunias, child with a balloon that must have been blue.

The last auction in Klinte: a reference book, a ship's compass,
a snus box with congealed froth. Leaves rained down onto the picture
of the pale green empress and so summer was over.

A clandestine chill in October. The rosehips are shriveled
like fingertips. The moon is a half-eaten crust in the sky.
Sheep in sparse flocks, inexplicably tattooed in purple.

It is autumn, the birds brace themselves against the gale.
The leaves fall like pages in a book where the glue has dried.
They will never be gathered again and read.

The trunk rot burns slowly after we have lit the compost.
In the earthworm humus there is movement as when stamps
loosen from their mountings. There is an underground realm.

Unexpected stop on the ferry line. People take their baggage,
step down into low grass. Flat country. A silo, a water tower.
Nothing stirs in the evening. They begin to believe they have arrived.

OTHER LIVES

He loved secrets—and revealing them!
So he became a storyteller. He wanted to be the black
box. The one they find after the disaster.

He owned a book from Voltaire's library that he had
never read. It lit up his existence like birthday illumination.
It consisted of purest bliss.

He stood at attention within himself. His chest held
a crowd in check. Invisibly bowing he drew
back inside a skin of sealed loneliness.

He was a traveling salesman in hesitation, the desire on low heat,
absent-minded compliments. His Sleeping Beauty with tight braids
he kissed with lips so dry she fell asleep anew.

With a leather-covered cell phone, he set out on travel by theme
to the pyramids, kept up with the low pressure areas in Singapore.
He became just a remote control, fucked only on the Internet.

He was a great teacher. Those who sat farthest back
didn't always hear what he said. But they worked out what they'd have
    said
in his place. So they were self-taught in the best of schools.

They lived in a sun yellow house, she in her sweat suit fixing
her hair every other step. Her husband chewed on Fussy Duddy
beef jerky. Their conversation, long drawn out like asparagus.

She walked sadly leaned forward: a figurehead
that had come loose from the stem of a ship
interminably greater than herself.

She left behind bills stained with
cooking oil, shriveled crab apples, sun-bleached
bags of purgative tea. Somewhat bitter, inconsolable.

She was given iron pills for sudden fainting. Verdi's notes
released her from the flesh's chains. Her spirit hovered
over the marshlands, free as a beach comber.

Well-bred as in a photo by Jaeger, pearl necklace and lace collar.
Her eyes pallid as tears. But on her sleeping body
he found traces of bird feathers and wild fur.

She cut off her braids and stuffed the pillow with them.
She hid her childhood out of sight. Out of dream's desk drawer
she pulled six brittle cat corpses, dressed in suit and bow tie.

On her breast she tattooed a cherub that flew when she lifted
her arms. Like a window washer her boyfriend glided
with his camera over her white body of glass.

His fingers drilled into her back.
She was wild with desire to go down deep
where she no longer saw him.

He examined her body with his third eye
just as he searched for the missing
thread of fiber in a forged bill.

They chewed their way through mealtimes, greedily reserved.
A horniness they never interpreted twined them into each other.
They were two shadows that lapped each other's milk.

They were seventy and lived in separate sun hats.
They knew the school reader (part 3) by heart.
Feelings flew between them on short wing beats.

—On the weekend he was a flooded campground in August,
during the week a very cold summer cottage. Each Friday I got a
    love letter
in an official envelope from the office of audits. I deceived myself
    with him.

She smelled of honey rose. Smiling sourly, too frail
to be touched, she munched chocolates filled with three
liqueurs. Her hairdo was a candied chestnut.

Once: the course around Lake Siljan on a motorbike with a sidecar.
    Now:
a walker to the TV room. To the girls who change catheters:
"Heaven is a house built without permit, get it? Show me a zoning
    plan!"

In school he always stared at the floor. Was considered shy
and ill-bred. "Look me in the eyes, boy!" But the stones
and Earth were silent. As geologist, he became world famous.

She laughed at statistics and paid tribute to the unpredictable.
Put stamps on crooked. She fought system builders and clean living
    people
with makeshift. The important thing was that nothing added up.

One day his wife found him on the floor. He was scouring
the sunshine with a nailbrush. The whole world should be washed.
The planks, transparent as ice, exposed the kingdom of the unborn.

Mirrors of Time

In 1934 Hitler gave orders for the black circus workers in the reich to
  be sterilized.
Fuck and kill! I read on the skinhead's T-shirt. The foreigners are best
oven-baked. From Klippan to Kungälv, Crystal Night sparkles.

A letter from Robben Island took a decade to arrive:
it was about albatross and hailstorm, about the South Pole, which
  moves
45 cm per year. A science program that censorship never broke.

In the spring weather I take a walk from the Islamic meat store
to Abdullah's shoe repair shop. The ethnographers are abolished.
The investigation of the Foreign happens most easily on the block.

Morning in Vasapark. The joggers adjust their headbands. The sun
fringes the fog. A blood filled needle in the gutter. The façades
still averse to light, and time a chokehold. Soon Ritorno's will open.

A flute solo drowns out the subway. The girl from
the music college tests how far the note reaches. People
walk past with their Walkman. Her beret is empty.

I like the seagulls that migrate to Döbelnsgatan
in June. Like colonels in the past, they strut oustide the French
school, Smörkringlan, the porn theatre and Hotel Come.

The workwear shop has become Boutique Gala. The confectioner's
sells candies in bags. My old haberdasher's is Solarium Vivåga
But near Zinkensdamm buttercup grows as before and sweet briar.

The streets were channels for rock music. Beer cans spurted.
The crossings were lit up by ads for Benetton.
The morning came, alone, ether sharp like an emergency ward.

Faded honeysuckle rubs against the windowpane. Across the garden,
uncannily enough, a person approaches whom I took as a deduction
on a tax form. I believed he was a loss I wrote off at 75%.

How's it going? A finger in the pie. A sharp eye on. All eyes.
Nose in someone's business. Hair on end. Backside in the air.
Turned tail. Heart in the mouth. Quite okay, actually.

A rusty bicycle outside an empty ministry on Sunday,
beer can on the transformer this evening when desolation
smells of week old milk: Open along the broken line.

The advent lights burned year round in the Baptist home for lost
girls at Regeringsgatan 93. Their lustrous hair was clipped short.
And equally short, their road from a broken condom to Jesus'
    embrace.

The private passions are played out on public notices now.
The public's marble friezes are corroded in a day.
Only humans without clothes have pockets to hide themselves in.

The municipality was placed under interim administration.
The regiment became the textile college, and the barracks the IT
    center.
The professor of gender studies' flute sounds from the residential
    district.

The Maranatha tent swells and stiffens in the spirit's storm.
The girls rosy as the pads of feet, innocent as milk.
From the preacher, the words drop down into God's own Melitta
    filter.

Töreboda in November. The coffin factory. Salon Barbro.
Taxi. ABF. Pära and Selma's Café. With a click
of the remote, Annette listens to a radio course in Italian.

Everyone jogs past my front door, I don't get the peace of the living.
She with the bright canine teeth gave me a costly look
and from her bare shoulder rose a butterfly in ink.

Alone with the cooked fish: there's no one else in the building.
Semi-matte vacation postcards make it hard to guess the weather
over chlorine scented pools where the children pee in secret.

Sweden is a captain's cabin. The supplies still ample.
We rock in the swells from a delayed future. The anchor
drags in the bottom mud. The imagination unemployed.

Afterhours at the stock exchange are over: receding trend. Smells
of meadowsweet and unripe blueberries. Our country: a cowhide
    covered
with gold leaf. Millions of unborn out there have already begun to
    hate us.

The future can't be seen. The present can only be observed locally.
Out in space it is Sunday a hundred thousand years ago.
At noon humanity goes to lunch.

No lover caresses breast and vulva, penis and thigh so carefully
as the blind in the Rodin Museum. Bodies that the chisel
has freed from the marble breathe under seeing fingertips.

In the Natural History Museum in New York, a flute is preserved
that's ten thousand years old. Where I walked the halls, the flute
from the ice age was playing, the moraine's light, clear as glacier water.

DEATH

Dying is like taking a final step into the air.
The paralysis lets go. Time stops climbing
like a mad ape on your back.

The present is the windowpane between dream and memory. Through it
a light ray travels, bent by Einstein. We exchange passion for
the memory of passion. Death is not the threat. But the unlived is.

Oarlocks creak on a still body of water. A row boat
approaches unseen. No wake, no reflection.
Transparent, it glides through everything that has been lost.

One evening with an unexpected power failure. An important page
I can't read is scanned by a domesticated insect.
The stars, the Shona say, are the eyes of the dead.

The windshield wiper goes slower than before.
I lean nearer to the glass to see.
If you could choose your death as you choose a lane to drive in.

The day has an icy edge of dismissal.
The exit is evident: not justice, not mercy.
Yet I don't believe that it was just a dream.

A moment's light, then an undisturbed darkness.
Soon we are dispersed. The stone returns to the fire.
Nothing ends though everything discontinues.

When she died, her photo faded and a twisted thread was seen
    blowing
through the window. An ink bottle screwed tight to have for the trip
began to leak. Seed cases opened for an urgent wind.

Final Departure Lounge: aperitif with tired truths.
Waitress with hectic red cheeks. An ape-like waiter,
vacuum dried variant of the undersigned, comes with the bill.

Old men who play chess seldom take their eyes from the board.
Their features tighten like before a lesson learned by heart.
Death leans imperceptibly over them. But they don't have time.

Dead friends are like fish, cross-striped in the morning light,
in a second swallowed up by the shadow. Potsherds remain
in dry river beds, the burned dung, coins in newly plowed fields.

Everything we've lost in the course of life vanishes in the big hopper:
the bandy ball, the ring, the book with addresses. We are united there
finally with everything we've lost. Others take over what we've saved.

I think I've been dead for a year, but still here like a poplar seed
in the house's chinks to cause an imperceptible settling. She bakes
bread for someone else. Everything moves on, they don't expect me back.

Just when the party's over, we get to know the names of the guests.
Just when the doors have been closed, we see the rooms expand.
When all the sounds have been turned down, we hear the spider webs sing.

Like when you let go of a load of wood and pull off an icy glove.
The stone table's slab wears even more, the erogenous zones shrink.
But the alphabet still glows, like asteroids over the expanses of snow.

August Nordenskiöld—Gustav the Third's Alchemist

Was it chance's grace, a frostbitten fable about goodness?
Backlight filled the bridge's arch from below. A chestnut slept in the
    leaves.
The mountains peaceful. The times permeated each other.

I flowed over my banks, had no shore to keep to.
Light doesn't see into darkness. The mosquitoes flew high over the
    cattle's spring.
The nightingale sang in its gloom when I went to meet the
    incomprehensible.

A dove's neck feather blew into the kitchen where I was grinding
    oyster shells
with a cave bear's canine. The insects screeched in the fire. The
    beautiful's
opposite is the sublime, which cannot be rendered, therefore not
    cited.

In the constellations I read forgotten abbreviations.
The churchyard smelled of smoke from a fire. The sky was melted
    metal.
O deceptive depth of mirrors, o infamy and collapse!

I laid out how the darkness that everything earthly takes part in
becomes knowable first when it resembles air and then
visible under name of water or earth.

Fell into disgrace with the upper school board when I explained
how an offspring of the invisible light bathes in five-fold
distilled liquid, in the Quintessence of all highness' power.

I went crestfallen out to the pansies. The grass stood white-haired,
the drinker's tongue white-striped. Each feeling's sweetness smothered
    by the soul's
and colleagues' torpor and my clamorous disciples. Night-long
    quicksilver wind.

Fluid red earth, brought to rest, fireproof with three essentials –
The Breath of something tough and elastic, the Water of a moist
    solvent,
the Blood of a fatty coagulant—becomes one fatty substance shining
    in the darkness.

The sauna was heated 11 January 1787. The sublimations more and
    more beautiful:
saw a fig tree, a globe. Smell of bread and eggs. Innocentia.
'The philosophical fire' burned forth in the gold a whitish blackness.

An unknown painter lingers among us. Even the stones have their ear
    canals.
But your eyes, my king, are as blind as cultured pearls.
The truth is the tears that make my writing paper buckle.

ANDERS SPARRMAN—CIRCUMNAVIGATOR, STRANDED

Mr. Linnaeus, my master and friend, called my language showy;
I reveled in whims, shunned nature's clear laws.
He recommended to me a monograph on the earthworm.
Enervated, I heard the air echo with laments.
A planet observed me with its Cyclops eye. The moon hunchbacked.
There was a smell of inherited clothes altered at night when the
      children slept.

Early, I suspected a sea-light in the yard's well.
I let the meanings sink to the bottom until the waters
became transparent anew. Thought: We are containers
for those we love, they are spirits inside our glass, they respire there.

At False Bay, tutor to the Dutch governor's son,
I mapped out the foundation of matter's internal character.
It contained the visible light and the inherent light,
which are bound with a beam of glory.

The orangutan's hour-long silence and the lion's low C,
the marabou stork in moth-eaten peace, the raven in a prosecutor's
      cowl
bent over the slave register: they reside in me still.

Antarctic icebergs—I was the first to see them—rose within me:
like absence of grief. My lead line broken. Feeling went out
on foreign seas. Death of others pressed inside me.

I offended myself when I wanted to breathe happiness. I sought
a flavor that didn't taste of me. I weighed anchor from the
      Resolution's
moorings and became a semaphore telegraph at humanity's fringes.

At the von Carlson house in Mälby, I shut myself into the aviary:
a wild bird, soon stuffed, a golden oriole lifeless.
When I depicted my sisters in misfortune in the republic of God
with a drawing pencil, I was attacked by a ram with a night jar
between its horns. Emanuel in my Museum Carlsonianum?

Doctor to the poor in Klara parish, I transmitted the stars' fluid
by mineral magnet to the shoemaker with scars of dog bites and
to the burned smith whose forehead shone like doors of a tiled stove.

The same substances unite us under a shifting sky
but can't flow down freely, only ooze forth
from upper reality – just as dye finds its way into
not yet impregnated cloth; otherwise, movement and cure cease.

I relinquished rest in the bosom of the family, the cigar's dark scent,
wreathes of the academies and the cheer from the fortress.
I came too close to things, people, Captain Cook.
I have seen more than I need to. I stumbled over the boundary
to myself and found myself on a village street in the universe.
Detours are necessary. Of straying from the path I've had enough.

In Cape Town I said to Thunberg: Life is a difficult
piece of music, a carelessly jotted score. He answered:
Under heaven's burnt vault speaks the One whose voice
lacks intonation and whose face cannot be described.

My severe, impatient master couldn't wait for me
who dawdled by an unwashed window at sundown.
But he taught me: "Finding is different from retrieving.

When reality takes a step forward,
the colors grow dense. No thinning agents!
For this reason our journeys do not end."

But the traveler stops traveling.